pamela mostek

blended

quilts with a creative edge

borders

Martingale®
& COMPANY

Mission Statement

Dedicated to providing quality products
and service to inspire creativity.

Credits

President & CEO: Tom Wierzbicki

Editor in Chief: Mary V. Green

Managing Editor: Tina Cook

Developmental Editor: Karen Costello Soltys

Technical Editor: Ellen Pahl

Copy Editor: Sheila Chapman Ryan

Design Director: Stan Green

Production Manager: Regina Girard

Illustrator: Adrienne Smitke

Cover & Text Designer: Shelly Garrison

Photographer: Brent Kane

Blended Borders: Quilts with a Creative Edge
© 2009 by Pamela Mostek

That Patchwork Place® is an imprint of
Martingale & Company®.

Martingale & Company
20205 144th Ave. NE
Woodinville, WA 98072-8478 USA
www.martingale-pub.com

Printed in China

14 13 12 11 10 09   8 7 6 5 4 3 2 1

**Library of Congress Cataloging-in-Publication Data
is available upon request.**

ISBN: 978-1-56477-930-4

contents

thinking
outside the borders

I am a fabriholic—a true fabric lover who can't bear to slice and dice fabulous fabric into little pieces to create a quilt. I'm always on the search for new and exciting ways to use today's gorgeous prints that are simply too beautiful to cut up into little pieces.

And I'm thrilled to tell you that I've come up with a fabulous new idea to share with you in this book. It's what I call a thinking-outside-the-box idea. Or, perhaps more accurately, a thinking-outside-the borders idea!

As in my earlier books, this book focuses on fantastic fabric and how to use it, but with a new twist. The twist is in the borders. It's all about adding a little pizzazz to this last step in putting together our quilts. Rather than the ho-hum style we often use to tack on those last strips of fabric, in this book you'll learn how to create an exciting border that will become the dramatic focus of the quilt.

In my quiltmaking history, I know that at times I've been in such a hurry to see it all done that I've settled for a border that was just an uninspiring add-on. Does that sound familiar to you? If it does, then the blended-border technique is a tool you can use to change that. With the right fabric, your borders can become the focus of your quilt, adding a truly showstopping finish to whatever quilt center you've pieced.

Just how do we do that? It's very simple. We begin by cutting out motifs from a large-scale print border fabric and positioning them in a pleasing manner on the border seam. They are stitched down during the quilting process using a raw-edged appliqué technique. The effect is to blend the quilt center and the borders without the usual straight seam line that separates them. The results are dramatic.

In this book you'll find step-by-step instructions for this technique, a sampling of projects you can create, plus a gallery of quilts using my blended-borders idea. As you will discover after viewing the quilts, this border technique can be used to enhance any quilt. All you need is a fabulous border fabric and you're ready to think outside the borders!

Enjoy!

My best,

Pam

blending the borders

The technique is simple but the results are amazing! It's a simple-to-do border treatment that will take your quilts from ordinary to extraordinary. It's all about cutting motifs from your border fabric, positioning them in a pleasing arrangement on the seam between the quilt center and the border strips, and then using raw-edged appliqué to stitch them to the quilt, blending the quilt center and border. For me, the fun part is placing those motifs, whatever they are, on the border seam.

It's not about totally covering the seam all the way around. I simply add enough appliqué shapes to give the illusion that the border spills over into the quilt center. There are more details to come on this as we go through the technique, so let's get started exploring this fun and fabulous border idea.

THE FABRICS

Selecting the fabric is one of my favorite parts of the process. Remember, I'm a fabric lover so the search for the perfect choice is a joy for me. There are a couple of things to keep in mind as you look.

First, the scale of the print is very important. Generally speaking, the bigger the better! Luckily, there are lots of fantastic large-scale prints on the market today, so finding the right one for your project shouldn't be too much of a challenge. In fact, narrowing your choices may be a bigger challenge! I usually look for prints that have motifs that are at least 6" to 8" across.

When I'm fabric shopping and I find a wonderful large-scale fabric that would be perfect for the technique, I buy it. Then I decide what I'm going to do with it later! Usually I buy about three yards when I don't know exactly what I'll do with it. Sometimes, if it's a totally drop-dead-gorgeous-once-in-a-lifetime print, I'll buy five yards. You'll probably find that large floral prints are the most abundant, but there are others. I've seen delicious-looking hamburgers, flying pies, juicy-looking fruit, fanciful fish, and many more. Remember to enjoy the hunt as well as your project!

When it comes to blended borders, ideal motifs measure from 6" to 8" wide or more.

Another detail to watch for when looking at fabric is the amount of overlapping motifs in the print. If all of the individual flowers or other objects in the fabric overlap each other, it's a little more challenging to use the fabric for this technique. Not impossible, just a little more challenging. We'll go over more details about cutting out motifs with an overlap in the section called "Cutting the Appliqués" on page 8.

Fabrics with overlapping motifs are harder to use in a blended border, but there are ways to make them work.

For each of the projects in this book, I've provided an estimate of the total amount of fabric needed so that you'll have extra fabric from which to cut the appliqués. Precisely how much you need varies depending on the scale and overlap of your print. It's always best to purchase a little more than you think you'll need. You can always add it to your fabric stash and use it for another project. If you add blended borders to a quilt design not from this book, don't forget to add in that extra yardage when purchasing the fabric.

PLANNING THE QUILT DESIGN

Now that you have the perfect fabric, let's talk about the actual design of the rest of the quilt. There aren't many rules here. Almost any design will work with this technique; however, for the most drama, your border should complement or even dominate the quilt. Remember, this is about spotlighting the borders. You wouldn't want to add blended borders to a stunning feathered star quilt center.

Making the borders the star of the show is easy to do with your fabric selection. Choose coordinating fabrics for the center that are not darker or brighter than your border fabric. Your quilt design can certainly include colors and shades from the border print; just don't throw in any that overwhelm the border fabric. Try the squint test. Arrange your fabrics into a fanned-out stack. Squint your eyes and look at the fabrics. If any of them pop out more than the border print, try something a little more subtle.

The scale of your border print will depend somewhat on the size of your quilt. A large bed-sized quilt will be the most effective if you choose a print with very large motifs. By large I mean a motif that's 10"–12" across. Prints of that size are out there—it simply might require a little more hunting!

Huge green leaves at the border balance the expanse of piecing in this bed-sized quilt.

A bold floral print accented with additional rose appliqués complements the simple pieced center of this quilt.

ADDING THE APPLIQUÉS

After your quilt is pieced and the borders added from your fabulous blended-borders fabric, it's time to add the appliqués.

Cutting the Appliqués

From your border fabric, cut approximately ⅛" beyond the outside edge of the motifs that you want to appliqué.

Cut motifs with well-defined edges by simply cutting ⅛" outside the desired motif.

If your print has overlapping motifs, again cut approximately ⅛" beyond the desired shape, following the outline as best you can even when that means cutting through the overlapping motif. You'll see a bit of added color from the overlapping shape, but look at the overall design and cut the shape that you want.

Varying flowers and leaves are all candidates for appliqués. If your print has a variety of great motifs, use them all! Some prints have one motif; others have multiple sizes and shapes of potential appliqué shapes.

Positioning the Appliqués

For best results when adding appliqués, put the quilt top on a design wall. If you don't have a design wall, a large piece of batting or a flannel sheet tacked or taped to the wall will work fine. This will allow you to step back to view your design as you work so you can place the appliqués where they look best.

Onto the border seam, begin positioning and pinning the cut-out appliqué shapes. Some of these can be placed on the seam where a flower or other shape has been interrupted as the border strips were cut and added. I like to use glass-head silk pins for this because they slide into the fabric easily.

Position appliqués over the border seam.

Add appliqués where there are open spaces in the print or plain areas along the seam line.

Often after I've added the appliqués along the seam, I find that I need to add a few on the border fabric itself to make a more pleasing arrangement, especially if the print is very symmetrical or the shapes are evenly spaced in a repeating arrangement. Adding a few additional appliqués in the border breaks up the spacing a little and creates a more interesting placement than if I simply repeat the spacing of the motifs in the fabric as I add the appliqué shapes.

Original fabric

Add a few additional appliqués on the border fabric. Vary the distance that the appliqués overlap beyond the border seam. You can even float a few completely into the quilt center.

Continue positioning and pinning the appliqués around the border seam. Adjust and move the appliqués until you are pleased with the arrangement. Don't forget to stand back and view your blended border from several feet back. It's amazing how that will help you to see what subtle adjustments need to be made to the positioning of the shapes.

Layer the quilt top with appliqué shapes, batting, and backing; baste. I prefer to use basting spray, but you may pin if that's your preference. Add a few more pins to the appliqué shapes, going through to the batting.

Pin appliqués in place, going through to the batting layer.

STITCHING THE RAW-EDGED APPLIQUÉS

Attach a free-motion quilting foot or darning foot to your machine and use a thread that blends with the fabric. Begin the raw-edged appliqué technique by adding a few stitching lines through the center of each appliqué shape, following the lines of the artwork of each. Next stitch around the outer edge of the actual appliqué piece, 1/8" inside the raw edge.

If you prefer, you may come back to the appliqués to add more decorative stitching once the rest of the quilt is quilted, but stitching them first will help secure them in place while you quilt the center. I typically don't embellish the appliqués because I want them to look the same as the border fabric.

QUILTING AND FINISHING THE QUILT

Quilt the center as desired. If you've created the quilt center with a large number of pieces, an overall quilting design works best.

An example of an overall quilting design used at the quilt center

When you quilt the large-scale print borders, follow the lines of the artwork of the appliqués, just as you've done when stitching down the appliqué shapes.

Outline the designs in the fabric when quilting the borders.

Add the binding, and your blended-borders quilt is complete.

Rough It Up

Remember this is a raw-edged-appliqué technique. The edges of the appliqués are meant to fray, adding dimension and interest to the design. I often use a toothbrush to rough up the edges of the appliqués after the quilting is complete.

simply **sensational**

Here's the perfect project to try out the blended-borders technique—it's quick and easy to make. This small wall quilt not only uses the technique for the borders but also uses it in the center square. The blended center creates a fabulous focus and is a great partner to those fabulous borders!

WHAT YOU'LL NEED

1½ yards of large-scale floral print for the center, appliqués, and outer border*

⅜ yard of coordinating print for the corner triangles

⅜ yard of coordinating small-scale print for middle border

¼ yard of coordinating small-scale print for inner border

⅜ yard of fabric for binding

1⅛ yards of fabric for backing

37" x 37" piece of cotton batting

Exact yardage amount may vary depending on your print.

CUTTING THE PIECES

From the large-scale floral print, cut:
1 square, 12½" x 12½"

2 strips, 4½" x 23½"

2 strips, 4½" x 31½"

From the corner-triangle fabric, cut:
2 squares, 9½" x 9½"; cut each square once diagonally to make 4 triangles

From the inner-border fabric, cut:
2 strips, 1½" x 42"; crosscut into:
    2 strips, 1½" x 17½"
    2 strips, 1½" x 19½"

From the middle-border fabric, cut
3 strips, 2½" x 42"; crosscut into:
    2 strips, 2½" x 19½"
    2 strips, 2½" x 23½"

From the binding fabric, cut
4 strips, 2¼" x 42"

Finished quilt: 31" x 31"

PUTTING THE QUILT TOGETHER

1. Sew two of the corner triangles to opposite sides of the 12½" floral square. Press the seam allowances outward.

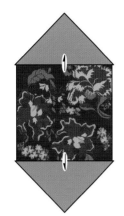

2. Sew the remaining triangles to the other two sides. Press. Trim to 17½" x 17½".

3. Sew the 1½" x 17½" inner-border strips to the sides. Press. Sew the remaining inner-border strips to the top and bottom. Press.

4. Sew the 2½" x 19½" middle-border strips to the sides. Press. Sew the remaining middle-border strips to the top and bottom. Press.

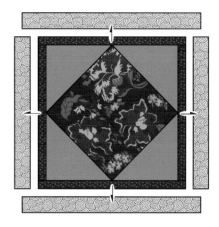

5. Sew the 4½" x 23½" floral strips to the sides of the quilt. Press. Sew the 4½" x 31½" floral strips to the top and bottom. Press.

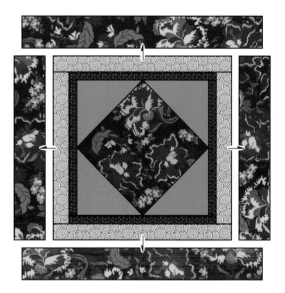

CREATING THE BLENDED BORDERS

1. To add the raw-edged appliqués and create the blended borders, refer to "Adding the Appliqués" on page 8. Referring to the photo, add appliqués to the seam between the center square and side triangles to create a blended look in the center as well as the borders.

How Many Appliqués?

Good question! It depends on the size of the quilt and the size of the print. Since this quilt is quite small, I used only a few added appliqués because I didn't want them to overwhelm the rest of the quilt—just enhance it. Try adding a few at a time and standing back and seeing how it looks. You'll know when you have enough.

Border seam →

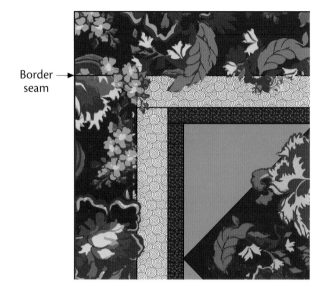

2. Refer to "Quilting and Finishing the Quilt" on page 11 to finish the quilt.

cinna**bar**

Circles are an absolutely no-fail technique for creating a dramatic quilt. Combine them with beautiful blended borders and the result is even more striking. With its deep browns and rich reds, this one will be perfect in my dining room. Don't be afraid of the circle block—it's easy and the results are fabulous!

WHAT YOU'LL NEED

2 yards of large-scale print for the outer borders and appliqués*

2⅞ yards *total* of assorted coordinating prints for blocks

½ yard of print for inner border

⅝ yard of fabric for binding

4 yards of fabric for backing

58" x 70" piece of cotton batting

Heavyweight template plastic

Small (28 mm) rotary cutter (optional)

Exact yardage amount may vary depending on your print.

CUTTING THE PIECES

From the inner-border fabric, cut:
5 strips, 2½" x 42"

From the large-scale print, cut:
4 lengthwise strips, 6½" x 54"

From the binding fabric, cut:
7 strips, 2¼" x 42"

Finished quilt: 52" x 64" • Finished block: 12" x 12"

MAKING THE BLOCKS

1. Using a permanent marker, trace the patterns on pages 20 and 21 onto heavyweight template plastic. Cut out on the drawn lines with scissors.

2. You will need 48 pieces each of pattern A and pattern B. Position each template on an assorted-print fabric and cut around it carefully using a small rotary cutter. You may also trace around the template with a permanent marking pen and cut out with scissors.

3. Pair up a fabric A piece with a B piece cut from a different fabric. With right sides together, position the A piece on top of the B piece, placing a pin at both ends and in the middle.

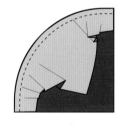

4. Using your ¼" presser foot as a guide, stitch along the curved edge as shown, easing slightly as you stitch.

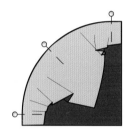

Use a Design Wall

Here's where working on a design wall will help you achieve the best layout for the scrappy circle blocks. After completing the blocks, position them in rows and stand back to check the placement. Move them around until you're pleased with the pattern created by the color shades.

5. Flip piece A so that right sides of the unit are up. Use your fingers to press along the seam line, pressing the seam allowance toward piece A. Don't use the iron to press at this point.

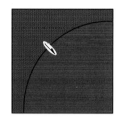

Finger-press along seam line.

6. Repeat steps 3–5 to make a total of four units for one circle block. Sew together in pairs as shown; then sew together the pairs to complete the block. Press carefully so as not to distort the block. Repeat to make a total of 12 blocks.

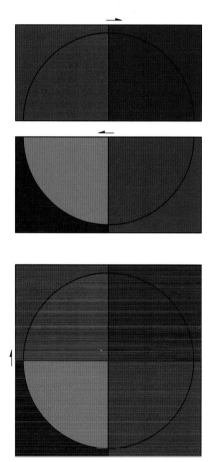

Make 12.

7. Arrange and sew the blocks into four rows of three blocks each. Alternate the pressing direction from row to row, and then sew the rows together.

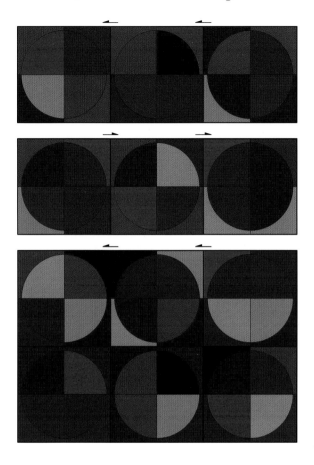

ADDING THE BORDERS

1. Sew the 2½" x 42" inner-border strips together lengthwise to make one long strip. Measure the quilt through the center lengthwise and cut two side border strips of that length from the long strip. Sew to the quilt; then press the seam allowances toward the border.

2. Measure the quilt through the horizontal center, including the side borders, and cut top and bottom strips to this length. Sew to the quilt and press.

3. Sew the 6½" x 54" outer-border strips together to make one long strip. Repeat the measuring process to add the side borders, and then the top and bottom borders. Press.

CREATING THE BLENDED BORDERS

1. To add the raw-edged appliqués and create the blended borders, refer to "Adding the Appliqués" on page 8.

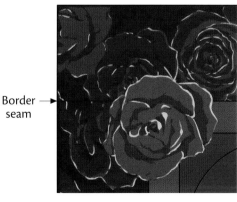

Border → seam

2. Refer to "Quilting and Finishing the Quilt" on page 11 to finish the quilt.

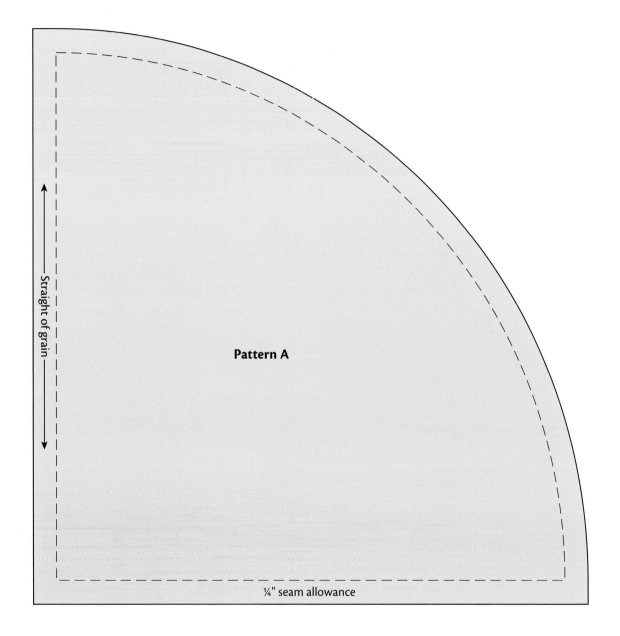

Straight of grain

Pattern A

¼" seam allowance

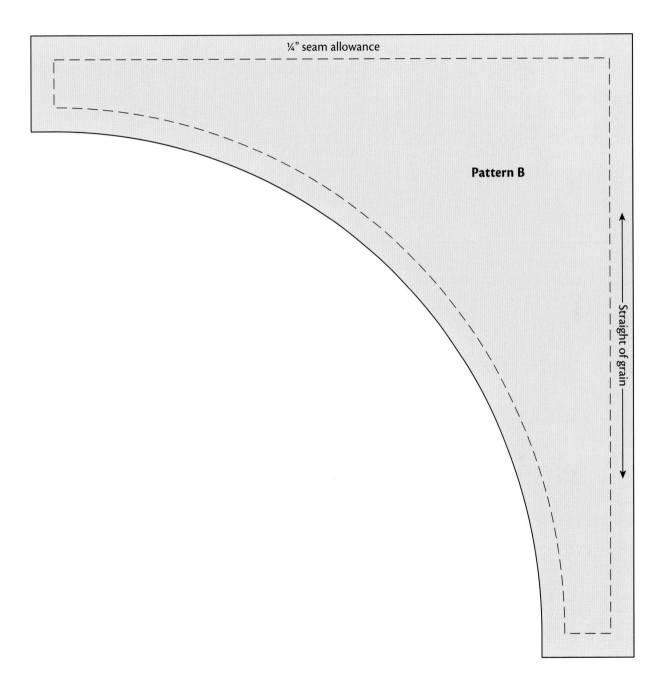

¼" seam allowance

Pattern B

Straight of grain

tropical **tango**

As soon as I found this absolutely WOW! fabric, I knew I had to use it in a blended-border quilt. The scale of the leaves is huge—some are even 12" in length. This makes it a real winner in the drama department! I combined it with one repeated block in the same colors to add to the blended look.

WHAT YOU'LL NEED

2½ yards of large-scale print for borders and appliqués*

3 yards *total* of assorted light to medium green prints in various print sizes and shades for blocks and setting triangles

1¼ yards of dark green print for blocks

⅝ yard of fabric for binding

5½ yards of fabric for backing

70" x 92" piece of cotton batting

Exact yardage amount may vary depending on your print.

The Size of the Quilt

Because this is a very large-scale print, I made the quilt proportionally large. The size of the quilt needs to be proportional to the size of the blended border you'll add to it. Appliqués of this size on a smaller quilt would have totally overwhelmed it.

Finished quilt: 61½" x 84" • Finished block: 8" x 8"

CUTTING THE PIECES

From the assorted light to medium green prints, cut:

39 squares, 2½" x 2½"

78 pieces, 2" x 5½"

78 pieces, 2" x 8½"

4 squares, 12⅝" x 12⅝"; cut each square twice diagonally to make 16 triangles

2 squares, 6⅝" x 6⅝"; cut each square once diagonally to make 4 triangles

From the dark green print, cut:

17 strips, 2" x 42"; crosscut into:

    78 pieces, 2" x 2½"

    78 pieces, 2" x 5½"

From the large-scale print, cut:

7 strips, 8½" x 42"

From the binding fabric, cut:

8 strips, 2¼" x 42"

MAKING THE BLOCKS

1. Sew a 2½" assorted green square between two 2" x 2½" dark green pieces. Press. Sew 2" x 5½" dark green pieces to the top and bottom.

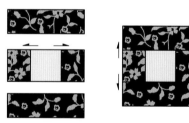

2. Sew two matching 2" x 5½" assorted green pieces to the sides of the unit from step 1. Sew 2" x 8½" matching pieces to the top and bottom. The block should measure 8½" x 8½". Repeat to make 39 blocks.

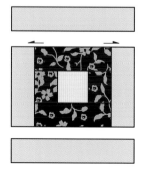

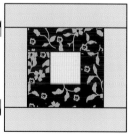

Make 39.

3. Referring to the diagram, arrange the blocks into diagonal rows. Sew the blocks into rows. Sew large side triangles to the ends of the rows as shown.

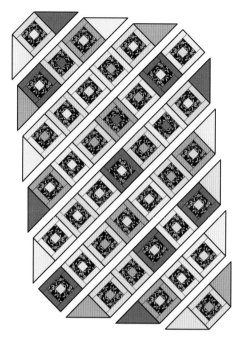

4. Sew the rows together and sew a smaller corner triangle to each corner.

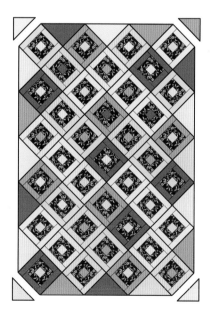

5. Sew the border strips together lengthwise into one long strip. Measure the quilt through the center lengthwise and cut two side border strips of that length from the long strip. Sew the strips to the sides and press the seam allowances toward the border. Measure the quilt through the horizontal center, including the side borders, and cut top and bottom strips to this length. Sew to the quilt and press.

CREATING THE BLENDED BORDERS

1. To add the raw-edged appliqués and create the blended borders, refer to "Adding the Appliqués" on page 8.

2. Refer to "Quilting and Finishing the Quilt" on page 11 to finish the quilt.

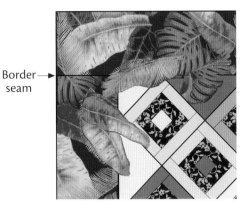

Border seam

On the blocks and setting triangles, quilted leaves echo the leafy border.

when **pies fly**

I couldn't resist this flying pie fabric! Not my usual fabulous floral, but I thought it was fun and was inspired to use it in a fresh kitchen quilt with blended borders. With its cheery, playful look, I can just see it on a kitchen table. Make it in a fabric with a different style, and it could be sophisticated, dramatic, or whatever you choose!

WHAT YOU'LL NEED

1¼ yards of medium- or large-scale print for the wide borders and appliqués

⅔ yard *total* of assorted medium red prints for blocks

⅝ yard of light print for blocks

⅝ yard of solid fabric for sashing

⅓ yard of print for narrow border

½ yard of fabric for binding

2 yards of fabric for backing

36" x 65" piece of cotton batting

CUTTING THE PIECES

From the medium red prints, cut:
8 strips, 2½" x 42"

From the light print, cut:
7 strips, 2½" x 42"

From the solid fabric, cut:
10 strips, 1½" x 42"; crosscut into:
    4 strips, 1½" x 27½"
    2 strips, 1½" x 34½"
    2 strips, 1½" x 29½"
    15 pieces, 1½" x 6½"

From the print for narrow border, cut:
2 strips, 2" x 32½"
2 strips, 2" x 36½"

From the medium- or large-scale print, cut:
2 pieces, 10½" x 32½"

From the binding fabric, cut:
5 strips, 2¼" x 42"

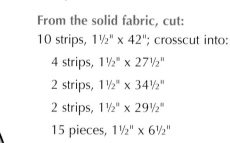

Finished quilt: 32" x 59" • Finished block: 6" x 6"

MAKING THE BLOCKS

1. Using the fabrics for the blocks, sew one light 2½" strip between two medium red 2½" strips and press. Make three strip sets and cut into a total of 40 segments, 2½" wide.

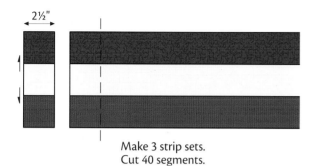

Make 3 strip sets.
Cut 40 segments.

2. Repeat step 1 to sew one medium red 2½" strip between two light 2½" fabric strips. Make two strip sets and cut into 20 segments, 2½" wide.

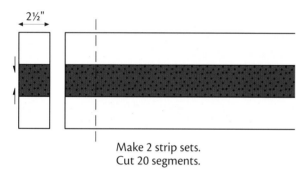

Make 2 strip sets.
Cut 20 segments.

3. Sew one segment from step 2 between two segments from step 1 as shown. Press. Make 20 blocks.

Make 20.

4. Sew three 1½" x 6½" sashing pieces and four blocks together to form a row. Make five rows.

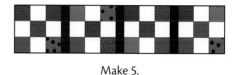

Make 5.

5. Sew four 1½" x 27½" sashing pieces between the rows as shown. Sew the 1½" x 34½" sashing strips to the sides. Sew the two remaining 1½" x 29½" sashing strips to the top and bottom.

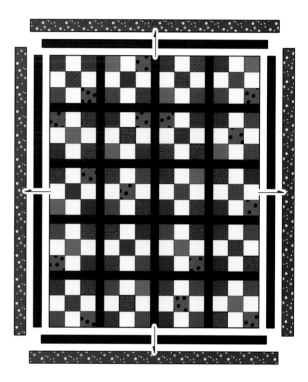

6. Sew the two print border strips, 2" x 36½", to the sides. Sew the two 2" x 32½" border strips to the top and bottom.

7. Sew the two large-scale print pieces, 10½" x 32½", to the top and bottom.

Just a Few Appliqués

Sometimes less is more, and this is one of those times. I added only a few flying-pie appliqués to the border seam, but I did add more pies to the wide border pieces in order to break up the even spacing in the original fabric. Putting in just a few appliqués there gave it more of a tossed, playful look.

CREATING THE BLENDED BORDERS

1. To add the raw-edged appliqués and create the blended borders, refer to "Adding the Appliqués" on page 8.

2. Refer to "Quilting and Finishing the Quilt" on page 11 to finish the quilt.

Border → seam

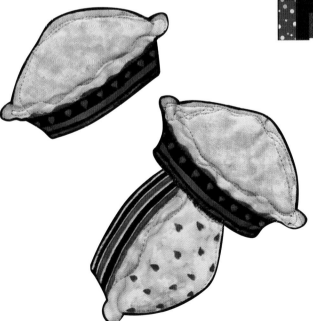

raspberry **mocha**

Delicate and delicious. That's the perfect description of this blended-border quilt. For a different touch, I added another straight border beyond the blended-border fabric so that both sides have the added appliqués. Definitely sweet enough to eat!

WHAT YOU'LL NEED

1¾ yards of large-scale print for border 3 and appliqués*

1⅛ yards of light geometric print for borders 2 and 4

⅓ yard of light print for blocks

⅓ yard of medium print 1 for blocks

⅓ yard *total* of assorted light prints for border 1

¼ yard of medium print 2 for sashing

¼ yard of medium print 3 for border corner squares

½ yard of fabric for binding

3½ yards of fabric for backing

57" x 57" piece of cotton batting

Exact yardage amount may vary depending on your print.

Choosing Coordinating Fabrics

Remember, to have your blended borders really pop, select the coordinating fabrics in shades and colors that won't dominate your border fabric. For this quilt I selected a soft pastel print on a cocoa-colored background. I choose the other colors in primarily lighter shades of the same colors so they would fade back and allow the blended border to shine.

Finished quilt: 51" x 51" • Finished block: 8" x 8"

CUTTING THE PIECES

From the light print for blocks, cut:
3 strips, 2⅞" x 42"; crosscut into 32 squares, 2⅞" x 2⅞"

From medium print 1 for blocks, cut:
3 strips, 2⅞ " x 42"; crosscut into 32 squares, 2⅞" x 2⅞"

From medium print 2 for sashing, cut:
3 strips, 1½" x 42"; crosscut into:

2 pieces, 1½" x 8½"

3 strips, 1½" x 17½"

2 strips, 1½" x 19½"

From the assorted light prints, cut:
2½"-wide rectangles of various lengths ranging from 3" to 8" (to total approximately 90")

From the geometric print, cut:
8 strips, 4½" x 42"

From medium print 3 for corner squares, cut:
8 squares, 4½" x 4½"

From the large-scale print, cut:
5 strips, 6½" x 42"

From the binding fabric, cut:
6 strips, 2¼" x 42"

MAKING THE CENTER

1. With a soft lead pencil, draw a diagonal line from corner to corner on the wrong side of the 32 light squares. Place each of the marked squares right sides together with a medium print 1 square. Using your ¼" presser foot as a guide, stitch ¼" from both sides of the drawn line on each square. Cut on the drawn lines to make a total of 64 half-square-triangle units. Press the seam allowances toward the medium triangles.

Make 64.

2. Arrange 16 half-square-triangle units from step 1 into four rows of four units each as shown. Stitch the units in each row together. Press the seam allowances in alternate directions from row to row. Sew the rows together and press the seam allowances in one direction. The block will measure 8½" x 8½". Repeat to make a total of four blocks.

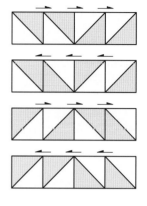

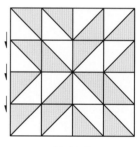

Make 4.

3. Sew a 1½" x 8½" sashing strip between two blocks from step 2 as shown to make a row. Make two rows.

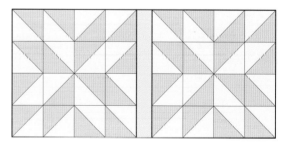

Make 2.

4. Sew the two rows together with the three 1½" x 17½" sashing strips as shown. Sew the remaining 1½" x 19½" strips to the sides.

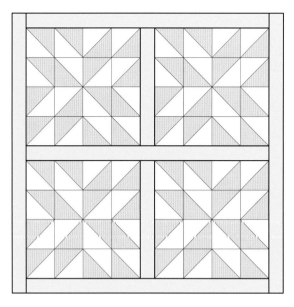

ADDING THE BORDERS

1. Sew the assorted 2½"-wide pieces together lengthwise into one long strip. From this pieced strip, cut two pieces, each 19½", and sew them to the sides of the quilt. Cut two pieces, each 23½", and sew them to the top and bottom.

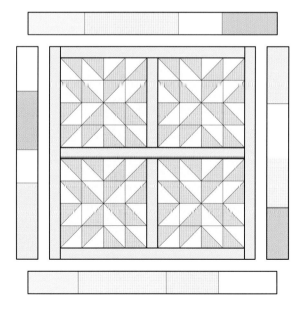

2. Sew three geometric print border strips together lengthwise into one long strip. From this strip, cut four 23½" strips. Sew two of them to the sides. Press. Sew corner squares to both ends of the two remaining strips and sew them to the top and bottom of the quilt.

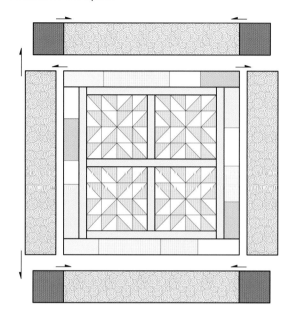

3. Sew the 6½" large-scale print strips together lengthwise into one long strip. From this strip cut two strips, each 31½", and sew to the sides. Press. Cut two strips, each 43½", and sew to the top and bottom.

4. Sew the remaining five geometric strips together to make one long strip. Cut four 43½" strips and sew two strips to the sides. Press. Sew corner squares to both ends of the two remaining strips and sew them to the top and bottom of the quilt.

CREATING THE BLENDED BORDERS

1. To add the raw-edged appliqués and create the blended borders, refer to "Adding the Appliqués" on page 8. Add appliqués to both seams on the sides of the large-scale print strip as shown in the photo at right.

2. Refer to "Quilting and Finishing the Quilt" on page 11 to finish the quilt.

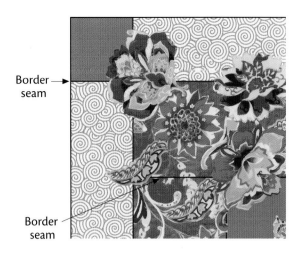

Border seam

Border seam

LAUREN'S LITTLE GARDEN by Pamela Mostek

Bursting with flowers, fruits, and vegetables, this quilt was made for my
granddaughter Lauren, who loves gardens, especially flowers. Adding just a
few blossoms to blend the border gives it more of that abundant garden look.
Sometimes it only takes a few appliqués to create the effect.

RASPBERRY ROSES by Pamela Mostek

"Flowers blooming everywhere" is the look I created by adding appliquéd roses to create a blended border. I also fussy cut the same flowers and included them in the pieced center. This is one of my favorite combinations of techniques!

ZINNIA PATCH by Carol MacQuarrie

When is a Log Cabin quilt more than just another Log Cabin quilt? When it's combined with a blended border, of course! Carol did a fabulous job of blending softer colors in a subtle pattern in the center, which allowed the brighter border flowers to really pop. Because her flower appliqués were large, she made a bed-sized quilt so that the borders wouldn't overwhelm the quilt.

TROPICAL PARADISE by Kathy Knox

Same Log Cabin block...but what a different result! In her quilt, Kathy used deep, splashy-looking batiks; for her blended border she choose a vivid orange floral that created a totally WOW effect! Matching the shade of the quilt center with the shade of the border fabric adds to the dramatic impact.

SUNSPOT by Pamela Mostek

One of my first blended-borders quilts, this is still one of my favorites. The simple pieced center drops back and allows the dramatic border of blended leaves to dominate the quilt. For more pizzazz, I stitched it with lots of metallic thread, and then added beads and crystals for the finishing touch. It was featured in my book *Dazzling Quilts* (Martingale & Company, 2006).

AUTUMN HARVEST by Amy Fitzpatrick

I love the golden autumn glow of Amy's quilt. It absolutely bursts with abundance, not only because of the harvest fabric she chose, but also because of the way her harvested crops spill into the quilt center. She also used some of her blended-border fabric in the pieced center, which adds to the overall warm look and feel of her delightful quilt.

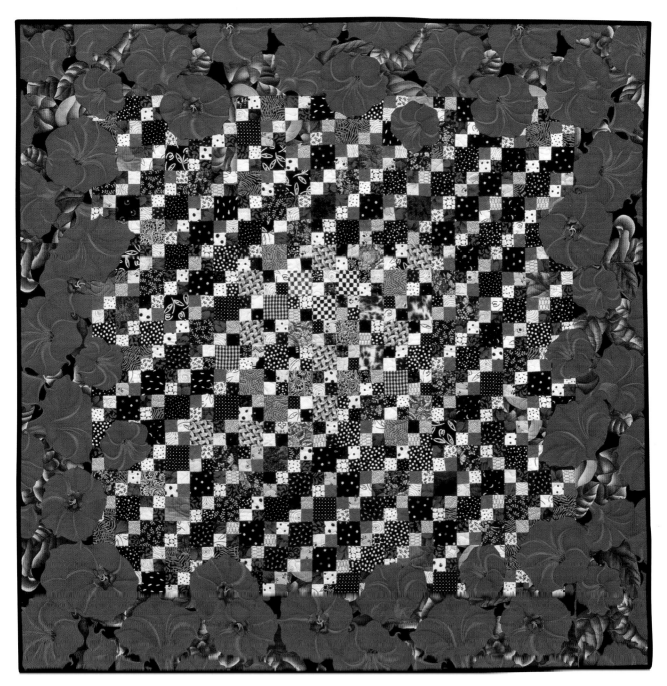

PATTI'S QUILT by Pamela Mostek

There's only one thing more dramatic than a black-and-white quilt, and that's one with a blended border of brilliant and beautiful red flowers. I have this category of fabrics that I call "once-in-a-lifetime-finds," and this fabric is definitely one of them. The quilt is from my book *Scatter Garden Quilts* (Martingale & Company, 2005) and is one of my all-time favorites.

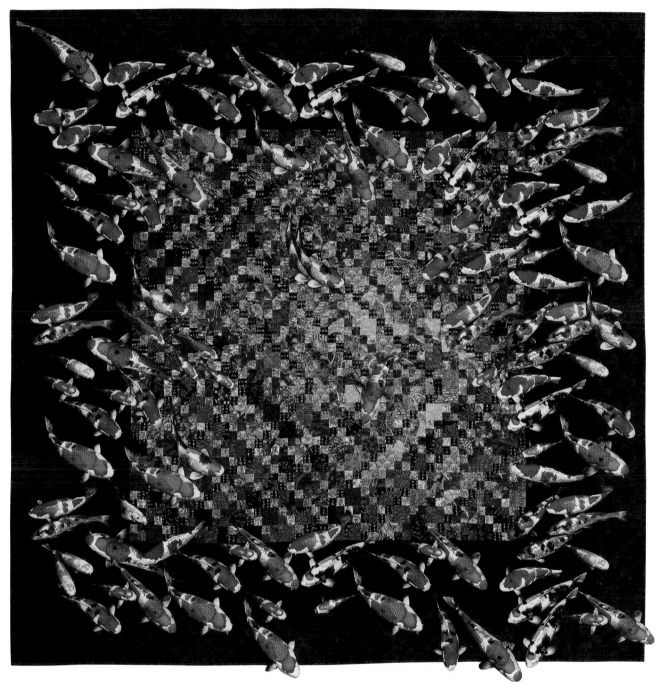

NOT SO SYNCRONIZED SWIMMING by Charlotte Freeman

Instead of large flowers, Charlotte used a print featuring koi, and the results are
fabulous. She did a superb job of creating movement not only with the swimming effect of her fish, but in the quilt center as well. Lots of extra effort went
into this lovely quilt; she created an original quilt that is truly outstanding.

STRAWBERRY SORBET by Pamela Mostek

Rather than my usual bold color palette, I used soft and subtle pastels to create a more delicate look in this quilt. My blended-border fabric had lots of overlapping motifs but I cut through the overlaps, following the line of my flower. I think that little bit of color on the edges of the leaves adds an unexpected touch of color. A very pleasant surprise! I created this quilt for a book I coauthored, *Quilt Challenge* (Martingale & Company, 2009).

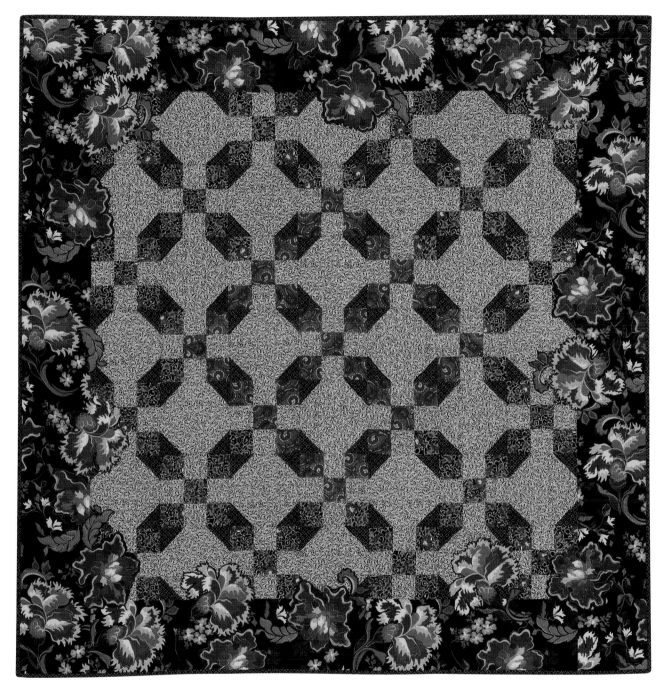

FRENCH GARDEN by Pamela Mostek

I love the vibrant colors of Provence, and I combined them with blended borders to create this quilt. Just a few overlapping flowers created that blended illusion. I designed "French Garden" for *Fons and Porter's Easy Quilts* magazine, and it is easy! What a great combination—easy-to-do and blended borders too!

acknowledgments

I'm very excited to bring this book of blended borders to you. Naturally and as always, I couldn't have done it without the help of a number of very special people. My deepest thanks go to:

Martingale & Company staff members, for their patience with me as I decided to do the book, "undecided" to do it, and then decided again to do it! I appreciate their faith in my ideas and their willingness to support them once again. They're the best.

My family…as always. My daughters, Stacey and Rachel, who are devotedly my best cheerleaders. I've said it before, but I'll say it again. They've always been my motivation for being a Mountain-Moving-Mom.

My husband, Bob. In spite of the fact that he tells me to "have fun" when I'm deep in the midst of writing, his faith in me is invaluable.

To my friend and seamstress Jean Van Bockel, for piecing the project quilts in the book. I'm so thrilled to have her talented and capable help.

To my friend and quilter Carol MacQuarrie, who once again added her expert quilting to my projects and brought them to life.

And to Bev Holmes, who willingly jumped into the process and added the bindings to the quilts. Welome to the team, Bev!

Those talented quilters who added their wonderful blended borders quilts to the gallery: Amy Fitzpatrick, Charlotte Freeman, Kathy Knox, and Carol MacQuarrie. Each quilt is uniquely different and shows just how versatile the technique can be.

To Bernina of America, for providing me with the fabulous sewing machine that makes it all possible. It's true nothing sews like a Bernina!

And lastly to my precious grandchildren: Jared, Lauren, Josie, and Brooklynn. Even though they don't know they're doing it, they constantly remind me of what is really important. It's only for them that I happily abandon my work and go off to play.

about the **author**

She'll freely admit it, Pamela Mostek is a true fabriholic, and she's especially passionate about large, dramatic fabrics drenched in color. Her ongoing search to find new ways to show them off is the inspiration for *Blended Borders*, her newest book dedicated to this goal.

Putting her degree in art and journalism to good use, she spends her time creating quilts for books and patterns for her design company, Making Lemonade Designs, as well as designing fabric, teaching, and making art quilts. Her work has been shown in many national shows as well as galleries. She is a proud mother of two grown daughters and four very special grandchildren. She and her husband reside in Cheney, Washington.

See more of Pamela's work at PamelaMostek.com.

New and Best-Selling Titles from

America's Best-Loved
Quilt Books®

America's Best-Loved Craft & Hobby Books®
America's Best-Loved Knitting Books®

APPLIQUÉ
Appliqué Quilt Revival
Beautiful Blooms
Cutting-Garden Quilts
Dream Landscapes
Easy Appliqué Blocks
Simple Comforts
Sunbonnet Sue and Scottie Too

BABIES AND CHILDREN
Baby's First Quilts
Let's Pretend
Snuggle-and-Learn Quilts for Kids
Sweet and Simple Baby Quilts
Warm Welcome—NEW!

BEGINNER
Color for the Terrified Quilter
Four-Patch Frolic—NEW!
Happy Endings, Revised Edition
Machine Appliqué for the Terrified Quilter
Quilting Your Style—NEW!
Your First Quilt Book (or it should be!)

GENERAL QUILTMAKING
American Jane's Quilts for All Seasons
Bits and Pieces
Bold and Beautiful
Country-Fresh Quilts
Creating Your Perfect Quilting Space
Fat-Quarter Quilting—NEW!
Fig Tree Quilts: Fresh Vintage Sewing
Folk-Art Favorites
Follow-the-Line Quilting Designs
    Volume Three
Gathered from the Garden
The New Handmade
Points of View
Prairie Children and Their Quilts
Quilt Challenge—NEW!
Quilt Revival
A Quilter's Diary
Quilter's Happy Hour

Quilting for Joy
Quilts from Paradise—NEW!
Remembering Adelia
Simple Seasons
Skinny Quilts and Table Runners
Twice Quilted

HOLIDAY AND SEASONAL
Candy Cane Lane—NEW!
Christmas Quilts from Hopscotch
Comfort and Joy
Deck the Halls—NEW!
Holiday Wrappings

HOOKED RUGS, NEEDLE FELTING, AND PUNCHNEEDLE
Miniature Punchneedle Embroidery
Needle Felting with Cotton and Wool
Needle-Felting Magic

PAPER PIECING
A Year of Paper Piecing
Easy Reversible Vests, Revised Edition
Paper-Pieced Mini Quilts
Show Me How to Paper Piece

PIECING
501 Rotary-Cut Quilt Blocks
Favorite Traditional Quilts Made Easy
Loose Change
Mosaic Picture Quilts
New Cuts for New Quilts
On-Point Quilts
Ribbon Star Quilts
Rolling Along

QUICK QUILTS
40 Fabulous Quick-Cut Quilts
Charmed, I'm Sure—NEW!
Instant Bargello
Quilts on the Double
Sew Fun, Sew Colorful Quilts
Supersize 'Em!

SCRAP QUILTS
Nickel Quilts
Save the Scraps
Scrap-Basket Surprises
Simple Strategies for Scrap Quilts

CRAFTS
A to Z of Sewing
Art from the Heart
The Beader's Handbook
Dolly Mama Beads
Embellished Memories
Friendship Bracelets All Grown Up
Making Beautiful Jewelry
Paper It!
Trading Card Treasures

KNITTING & CROCHET
365 Crochet Stitches a Year
365 Knitting Stitches a Year
A to Z of Knitting
All about Crochet—NEW!
All about Knitting
Amigurumi World
Amigurumi Two!—NEW!
Beyond Wool
Cable Confidence
Casual, Elegant Knits
Crocheted Pursenalities
Knitted Finger Puppets
The Knitter's Book of Finishing
    Techniques
Knitting Circles around Socks
*Knitting More Circles around
    Socks—NEW!*
Knits from the North Sea—NEW!
More Sensational Knitted Socks
*New Twists on Twined Knitting—
    NEW!*
Pursenalities
Simple Stitches
Toe-Up Techniques for Hand-
    Knit Socks, Revised Edition
Together or Separate